John Lautner™

Barbara-Ann Campbell-Lange

JOHN LAUTNER

1911–1994

Disappearing Space

TASCHEN

KÖLN LONDON LOS ANGELES MADRID PARIS TOKYO

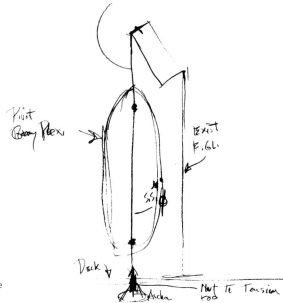

Illustration page 2 ▸ John Lautner on site
inspecting formwork prior to casting
Illustration page 4 ▸ A quick on-site sketch
explaining the transfer of forces in a perimeter
connection detail

©2005 TASCHEN GmbH
Hohenzollernring 53, D-50672 Köln
www.taschen.com

Editor ▸ Peter Gössel, Bremen
Project management ▸ Swantje Schmidt, Bremen
Design and layout ▸ Gössel und Partner, Bremen
Text edited by ▸ Susanne Klinkhamels, Cologne
Text revised for this edition ▸ Johannes Althoff,
Berlin
Proof-reading ▸ Wolfgang Mann, Sydney

Printed in Germany
ISBN 3-8228-3962-0

To stay informed about upcoming TASCHEN
titles, please request our magazine at
www.taschen.com or write to TASCHEN America,
6671 Sunset Boulevard, Suite 1508, USA-Los
Angeles, CA 90028, Fax: +1-323-463.4442. We will
be happy to send you a free copy of our magazine
which is filled with information about all of our
books.

Contents

Introduction

Left page:
Apprentices working outside at drawing boards, Taliesin West
Lautner is in the foreground.

"50 years have gone by and it feels like five or ten and I don't know what the hell happened because I was involved."[1]

John Lautner was a tall man with a generous smile, who looked good in red. His desk was always full of the things he was thinking about that day: a patterned shell, an image of an arching Egyptian goddess, a piece of text about the essence of beauty. On the wall was a photograph of the Arango Residence, so large one could almost step onto its open raw-marble terrace, held in timeless tension between sea and sky. His buildings still appear new and fresh, free of stifling references, and they hold a profound sense of belonging: to the place, the people and the architect. Cherished by all who knew him, Lautner has left a legacy of barely known work that speaks of the infinite potential of architecture.

For more than 50 years Lautner wrestled with the jarring commercialism and transitory infatuations of Los Angeles. His Hollywood office overlooked the fickle styles of what he called "real-estate fakery" crowding the hills, few of whose 10 million inhabitants were interested in his work. "Architecture is for people and that is forgotten. Most of it is for rent, for sale, for lease but not for people."[2] He said he "gave up the woods for a life of architecture", and one is aware within his houses of a search for the sensations of the primeval forest he knew as a boy.

Lautner's early projects embodied some influences of the work of Frank Lloyd Wright, with whom he had apprenticed at Taliesin. However, in time his work evolved a unique conception of architectural space, form and attitude to materials. This development is discernible through careful study of the plans and sections of his buildings; however, photographs—particularly of the interiors—convey only partial truths about the complex non-rectilinear spaces that they frame. Inevitably, as with all good architecture, it is only by visiting the buildings that Lautner's particular vision can be properly appreciated. And this is where his success—in the worldly sense—foundered: most of Lautner's work comprises private houses that are rarely accessible.

This inaccessibility, both physical and graphic, meant that Lautner did not achieve prominence amongst his peers or the architectural press during his lifetime—something that was both a personal disappointment and a deep frustration of his hopes for the future of architecture. This situation may have been exacerbated by the blockbuster movies in which some of his houses starred: Diamonds are Forever (Elrod Residence), Body Double (Malin Residence "Chemosphere"), Lethal Weapon (Garcia Residence), Less Than Zero (Reiner Residence "Silvertop"). Despite this, Lautner had a large and passionate following of free-thinking individuals, who packed his lectures, made pilgrimages to his office, and trespassed to his houses.

1 Cohen, Bette Jane: *The Spirit in Architecture, John Lautner.* Documentary film written and directed by Bette Jane Cohen, produced by Bette Jane Cohen and Evelyn Wendel, 1991.
2 Lautner, John: Lecture given at SCI-Arc Los Angeles, 23 January 1991.

Background

Born in 1911, Lautner grew up on the wild edges of Lake Superior in northern Michigan, where he discovered "the infinite variety of nature". Memories of contact with this landscape—the freedom of horizons, the patterns of the winds, the moods of the

Aerial view of suburban Los Angeles

water and the qualities of light filtering into undisturbed forests—were to echo within his work for a lifetime. In later life he often referred to the timelessness of this unspoilt place and sought ceaselessly to achieve its "basic life-giving qualities" in his architecture.

Lautner's mother was a painter, the designer of their holiday cabin, and the first in the family to read Frank Lloyd Wright's 1932 autobiography. His father, educated at several famous European universities, was a teacher by profession. At the age of 12 Lautner helped his father to build the family cabin on a rocky peninsula jutting out into Lake Superior. Together they rafted logs across the lake, and built a skidway up the mountainside. He learnt the mechanics of the windlass and the practicality of handling rough timber—physical contact that spawned an innate confidence in materials and making.

Lautner chose architecture as a career because he felt it involved everything in life and was therefore least prone to the boredom of ruts and routine. After college he was about to embark on seeing the world when he heard of Wright's unique training for architects. Scornful of conventional architecture schools—"All they do is grade on neat and to hell with the ideas"[3]—and having read Wright's autobiography, he decided to go to Wisconsin, where Wright had created a school for trainee architects during the Great Depression. He was accepted by Wright because he had undergone no previous architectural training and therefore had less to unlearn.

The Taliesin East school taught more than draughting. Physical labour such as stonework, carpentry or farm work was complemented at the weekends by Sunday evening dinners, sometimes with string quartets, when Wright would invite as many as 50 or 60 guests. The apprentices would plan, cook and wash the dishes for these events, absorbing the discussions and Wright's talk of the ideals of democracy. In this environment Lautner absorbed the idea of architecture as a whole, integral with life.

Lautner lived in the Ocotillo winter camp in preparation for the construction of Taliesin West, which he physically helped to build—hard physical labour, but exhilarating. It developed in him a fundamental understanding and respect for building, for people and for the landscape. Lautner discovered how to detail in a way that was not

The family cabin on a peninsula jutting out into Lake Superior

only suited to the nature of the material but also descriptive of the essence of an idea. "The basis of Mr Wright's work, which has been one of the main things I learnt from him, is that you have to have a major idea. If you don't have an idea you don't have architecture, and very few people seem to know that. They have combinations ..."[4]

Lautner deliberately avoided copying any of Wright's drawings or taking photographs. He already knew he wanted to develop his own philosophy, his own architecture. Wright supported this attitude. Despite this, few other apprentices broke free of Wright's influence.

Lautner worked with Wright for six years. While at Taliesin, he witnessed Wright creating "Falling Water" (1936). He later supervised the construction of Wright's Abby Beecher Roberts House, "Deertrack" (1936), and the Herbert Johnson Residence, "Wingspread" (1937). For the Johnson Residence Lautner managed an excellent crew of carpenters who were all cabinetmakers. The last two projects that Lautner supervised—the Sturges House (1939) and the Oboler House (1940)—brought him to Los Angeles. Overseeing the building of the Sturges House, Lautner obtained all the permits and arranged all the contracts. He knew that the more contracting experience he acquired the more he could achieve in his own practice. After completing the Oboler House, Lautner left Wright to start his own practice in 1940.

Method of Designing

Lautner's approach to architecture was instinctive and experiential, or—as he often described it—"a total involvement". He designed from the inside out. "It's thinking right from scratch and having a major idea, from inside. I've never designed a facade in my life."[5]

Lautner drew with the mind of a carpenter, building while he was drawing. His sketches were rough, loose and almost childlike, every mark with a reason and to scale. His initial freehand plans and sections indicate a clear sense of structure. Unlike much media-driven architecture, for him the drawing held no cosmetic importance; it was merely a tool of communication.

3 Cohen, op. cit.
4 Wahlroos, Ingalill: *John Lautner*. Unpublished interview for UCLA Architecture Journal, 29 November 1989.

5 Campbell-Lange, Barbara-Ann: *John Lautner*. Unpublished interview, 10 December 1990.

Frank Lloyd Wright, Gatehouse for Arch Oboler, 1940
The last two Frank Lloyd Wright projects that Lautner supervised, the Sturges House, 1939, and the Oboler House, brought him to Los Angeles.

The idea mattered above all else. The idea was unique to each client. Every house and every site was understood as a distinct challenge. He believed that the problem to be solved was how to create buildings that could grow and live with people without confining them—buildings that provided light, air and freedom, immeasurably enhancing people's quality of life. Lautner called this "Real Architecture".

Projects were often characterized by an iconic image or metaphor: for example a cave, terrace or roof (Segel, Arango and Sheats/Goldstein respectively). "I have the whole project in my head before I put it down on paper."[6] From this visualization Lautner would make a simple cardboard model to describe the flowing three-dimensional spaces he had conceived, as he found renderings misleading. The model communicated the spatial intentions of the design to his clients, and helped his architects to develop working drawings.

"My clients are all pretty strong individuals or they wouldn't come at all, they wouldn't be doing anything, they'd just do what the status quo said to do, the average. I don't have any average, no average at all."[7] A surprising number of Lautner's clients were involved in the construction of their own buildings, particularly the early smaller houses. As owner-contractors or owner-supervisors, clients Mauer, Gantvoort, Alexander, Deutsch, Harpel and Malin responded to his practical approach and peculiarly American pioneering ingenuity. Kenneth Reiner experimented with Lautner on new building systems in a workshop alongside his factory. Mrs Segel, commenting on Lautner's rapport with his clients, exclaimed: "We've been dancing together throughout."[8]

In contrast to his dismissal of most contemporary architecture, Lautner was familiar with the work of contemporary engineers such as Felix Candela and Pier Luigi Nervi. His architectural vision, combined with his appreciation of fine craftsmanship and daring structures, attracted gifted engineers, contractors and master-builders. It was these individuals who gave physicality to his ideas, making the impossible possible. Wally Niewiadomski, who realized most of Lautner's concrete buildings—specifically Elrod and "Silvertop"—and John de la Vaux, who built the Carling, Deutsch, Harpel and Malin Residences, are the two key characters in this respect. Both responded to the adventure of the projects, and to Lautner's keen eye for detailing and finishing.

"The creative process—it's a sweat. The thing is to be able to hold, and try to pull together, all the possible emotional elements, physical elements, structural elements and nature, and try to pull that into an idea. One idea. And you have to practise. So since I have been practising that way for 50 years I can do it. But I have better control now than I ever did."[9]

To define Lautner's work one needs to look at how the transition between inside and outside is made. The way he evolves this is non-linear and non-chronological; rather it is an elliptical exploration where techniques are revisited in new ways. The Private Residence (1990) represents the point in this cycle that Lautner had reached when he died in 1994. This development is characterized by a number of key projects.

Carling is representative of the projects where the floor is invested with the weight of transition. The floor is stepped, and collaged with differing materials, water, and internal planted areas, moving outside to include itself in the view. At Wolff the transfer between inside and out is moved from the floor to the wall, to the spaces between the stony walls and glazed interior. This zone is then compressed to the edge of the en-

6 Lautner, Lecture, op. cit.
7 Cohen, op. cit.
8 Escher Frank (ed.): *John Lautner, Architect.* Artemis London Limited, London, 1994, p. 203.
9 Campbell-Lange, op. cit.

Lautner set up his own office in Los Angeles in 1940.

Googies Coffee House, Los Angeles, 1949

velope, as seen in the faceted facade of the Pearlman Residence and the thickened angling edge detail at Malin.

At Garcia (1962) and Stevens (1968), Lautner internalized the entire interior under roofs that run perpendicular to the axis of the view. Walstrom (1969) is self-reflexive in another way, propped off the slope to look back at the path that gives it entry.

The main rooms of the bigger houses change from a thrust-forward position to the way in which it is supported between the curving accommodation wings of "Silvertop". At Elrod (1968) the main room sinks into the site, under the weight of the encapsulating concrete roof, the edge of which presents a cyclorama of landscape and sky. The room is an inverted lens to the landscape outside: black sky below, cupping earth above. The landscape has been drawn in.

The roof develops over the whole building. The Hope Residence (1979) was to have had an internal geography, while the roof of the Beyer Residence encloses rockpool-like areas that are wound around into the seashore. The main room of the Segel Residence is placed between the mountain-like promontory of the service accommodation behind and beach beyond, inscrutable below a grassy roof.

Depending on the circumstances of the project, the profile of floor or wall or roof determines the relationship between the individual and idealized nature. At Arango and Sheats the roof becomes the definitive agent of transition.

Conclusion

Although his architecture is sometimes termed "organic", Lautner eschewed this description in the narrowest sense because of its connotations as a Frank Lloyd Wright style. Rather than working to create an attributable image, his practice was concerned with what a building did rather than how it seemed. Academic classifications, in his opinion, were applied only to clichés.

"The term Organic architecture means more than just organized structure. It means the infinite variety of nature applied to spaces for human beings—indefinable, therefore alive."[10]

10 Wahlroos, op. cit.

Lautner's buildings are not literally of nature; rather they create a sense in the beholder, the inhabitant, which is like that of exposure to a natural force: "intangible essences". The result is, like nature, graduated from dark to light, from closeness to openness, and, as a landscape changes, Lautner's expression of this sense changes through his lifetime, from tent to cave.

Each work achieves Lautner's own patented peacefulness, conjured by being on the edge of a glorious view. However, it is the view as distant focus that makes it possible to develop within each building, from back to front, a temporary control over the inevitable movement of space to the outside.

Glazed facade and swimming pool are interlocutors in this balancing act, capturing, reflecting and allowing one to see beyond simultaneously. So too the changing weather conditions provide a varying perspective to the focus beyond. "Disappearing space seems to me to be the most durable and endurable and life-giving quality in architecture."[11]

Each surface is poised and its materials chosen to manage and prolong the suspense before that release; wherever you look you don't see a wall. Geometry is only servant to this suspense, the about to become. The unpredictable play of light and air

11 Pendro, Waymond James: *Solid and Free: The Architecture of John Lautner*. Unpublished thesis, University of California, Los Angeles, 1987.

Arango Residence, Acapulco, Mexico, 1973
Cardboard model

Left page:
Arango Residence, Acapulco, Mexico, 1973

Right:
John Lautner in his office on Hollywood Boulevard, 1990

that make serendipitous connections with surfaces all occurs in the now, giving all an ever-fresh sense of place.

"I choose not to be classified and remain instead continuously growing and changing, with basic real ideas contributing to life itself, for timeless enjoyment of spaces—which I call Real Architecture. No beginning, no end—always."[12]

12 Campbell-Lange, op. cit.

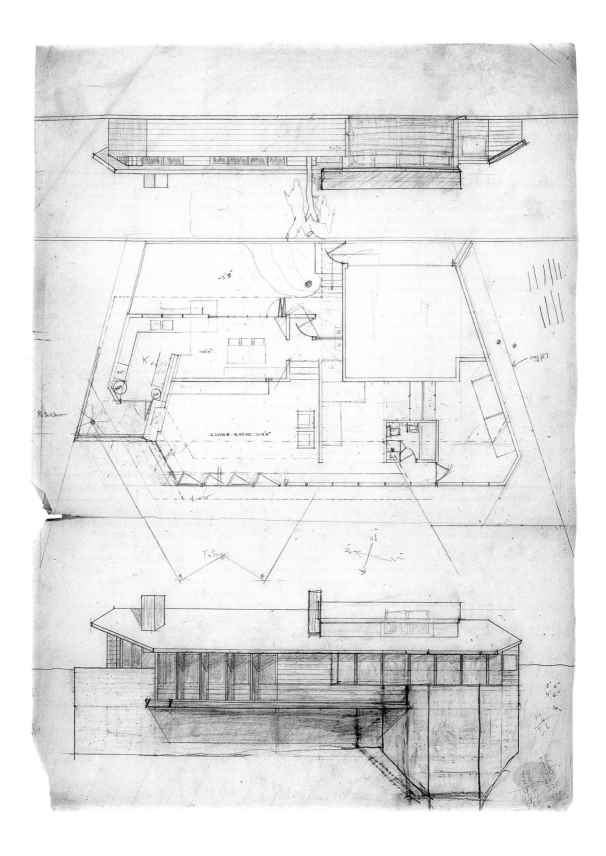

1940 ▸ Lautner Residence
Los Angeles, California

Instead of resorting to expensive retaining walls, the Lautner Residence (1940) is supported on steel beams and posts. These are screened by a stud wall, which makes this modest building seem surprisingly monumental when seen from below. It extends into the hillside at the back, creating a sheltered outside garden room. Each major space drops down a level following the site's contours, collected above by the embrace of the monopitch roof projecting into the view.

1946 · Mauer Residence
Los Angeles, California

The roof of the Mauer Residence operates in a different way. It is structurally independent of the walls, supported on a series of plywood bents, which were prefabricated and erected by a subcontractor to reduce costs. Dr Mauer supervised the rest of the work, filling in the space below where it was required. Parts of the living room and master bedroom rotate out from under the roof's rectilinear grid, letting in light unexpectedly to the fireside alcove from a clerestory opening. The intimacy of the alcove contrasts with the relaxed generosity of the main living room, which pivots through glass doors into the garden courtyard beyond. The interior is proportioned to suit its inhabitants, and its comfortable scale and materials do not dictate the position or choice of furniture. The independent roof structure at the Mauer Residence allows flexibility of enclosure below and makes a sloping ceiling assisting natural ventilation. The striped skylights create a softening light transition between inside and outside.

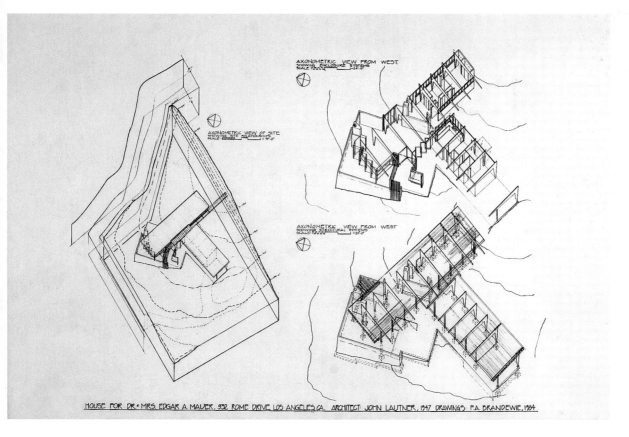

HOUSE FOR DR & MRS EDGAR A MAUER, 932 ROME DRIVE, LOS ANGELES CA. ARCHITECT: JOHN LAUTNER, 1947 DRAWINGS F.A. BRANDEWIE, 1984

The living and dining area with large pivoting
doors to the terrace

View from hall into the kitchen

Left:
Plan

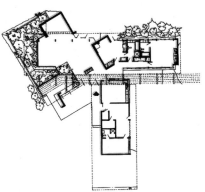

1947 · Gantvoort Residence
Flintridge, California

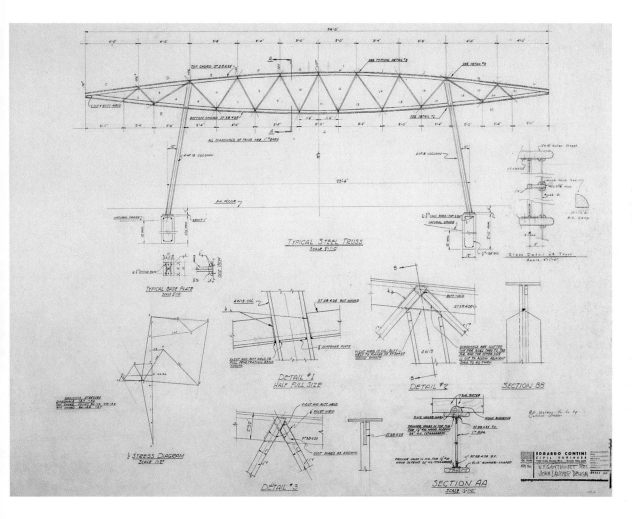

Final plan
Structural engineer Edgardo Contini's drawing for the roof structure of bowed lightweight steel trusses supported by inclined steel columns to take horizontal and vertical loads. Mr Gantvoort acted as contractor on the entire job.

The house was designed to suit Mr Gantvoort's collection of teakwood furniture from Java. Mr Gantvoort acted as contractor on the entire job. The house utilizes the same principles as the Mauer Residence with prefabricated, bow-shaped steel roof trusses. A wooden trellis provides lateral support at the bottom of the trusses and creates a shady perimeter.

Left page:
Living room looking towards bedroom wall

View from living room out to covered terrace

Exterior view at entrance to living room

Left:
Plan

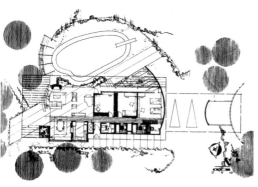

1947 ‣ Carling Residence
Los Angeles, California

A light hexagonal roof perches over the main living room space of the Carling Residence on tripod supports. The roof structure of the side wing marches to its own rhythm, while the walls, shelves and internal planting arrange themselves around the support columns, and articulate the roof edges with a dancing in-and-out line. The cadence of the steps, deck, pool and contours creates a contraction and release of space that moves from the outside with subtle gradations of level into the main living space, and then through to the partitioned-off private accommodation, all gathered by the anchoring shape of the hexagonal roof. Carling can be typified as creating a balance between introverted and flowing space, top-lit areas and where light pours in from full-height glass elevations held under the tent of the roof.

It is with sensitivity to this flow that Lautner has placed walls, changed material or opened up to a view, rather than in response to some abstract numerical imperative. This explains the lasting attraction of the places he made.

Outside, the roof works as a new hilltop, a built extension to the natural contours of the site. Inside, its strong form unifies the shifting shapes and changes in level. Lautner repeated this economical roof structure, eminently suited to sloping sites, for the Polin and Jacobsen Residences, both built in 1947.

Plan

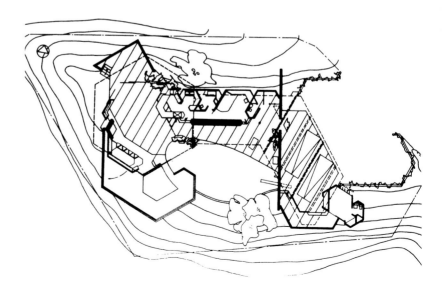

**Night view from across the pool looking into
the living and dining room**
The glass front wall of the living room has been
slid open and the wall-seat to the left pivoted out
to enjoy the uninterrupted 360-degree view.

View from raised level beside fireplace looking
out to view

1947 ▸ Desert Hot Springs Motel

Desert Hot Springs, California

Left page:

View of terrace
The roof overhang and high walls provide
protection from the desert winds and sun.

View from an enclosed terrace into a unit
Showing the angular steel external structure to the
suspended gunite roof-slab. The jagged shape of
the gunite walls makes them self-supporting.

Each small unit of the Desert Hot Springs Motel is made to seem bigger than it is by
the way in which space is coiled down into it through the skins of the enclosure and the
manipulations of the ground and roof levels. Cool top-lit spaces are made inside the
exoskeleton of jagged walls and spiky steel superstructure. The suspended gunite roof
slab angles open to the sky, seen through a clerestory. An inclination of the party wall
turns the space around, over a raised platform of turf for deckchairs, to meet the view.
The whole forms a protective line of defence in this harsh, windy environment, characterized by its low-lying silhouette, where the broken shapes of the steels of the roof
structure repeat the rhythm of the fissured mountain crags beyond.

View of the swimming pools

Exterior view of the Desert Hot Springs Motel
The roofs echo the fissures of the mountains
behind.

1949 ‣ Schaffer Residence

Montrose, California

View from outside terrace towards the living room

Redwood is used throughout. Two by eight redwood screens are used around the perimeter of the building as fence, siding or alternated with glass as for the kitchen wall.

Right:

Interior view towards the glass and timber wall of the kitchen and dining area

The screen on the left divides the passage from the living room.

The Schaffer Residence lies amongst the oak trees of a wooded picnic site frequented by the family. The internal spaces are sketched with a deft yet informal minimalism inside a compound described by redwood fencing. Daylight and sunlight penetrate through the gaps between the fencing boards, dematerializing its boundary.

The hourglass shape of the main space—part extrovert living room, part introvert walled garden—is produced by the accommodation wings levering in like a pair of scissors and the poised position of the fireplace. Space is pushed out to the sides of the chimney by the angling roofs above the kitchen and dining room, to views of trees and sky. The 2ft wide concrete strips of the formal entrance path become, at the end of the house, a playful forest-edge boardwalk. A congress of roofs, sliding past each other yet also somehow agglomerating, accentuates the atmosphere of a clearing in the forest.

Plan

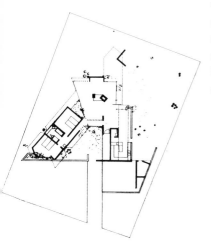

1950 ▸ Foster Residence
Sherman Oaks, California

Left page:

View from below

A covered terrace is located under the encircling roof.

Right:

Street elevation

The arrangement of the windows gives this elevation a scaleless quality.

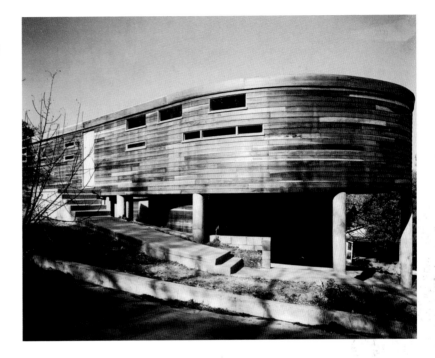

The Foster Residence stands on the hillside on concrete columns, again avoiding the expense of retaining walls, just touching the hill by the front door. It is difficult to ascertain the scale of the roadside facade, as the long strip windows hide themselves in the horizontal timber cladding, and the wall disappears around a curve at one end without a corner fullstop. By contrast the opposite side of the house opens up to expansive views of the landscape below.

The Foster Residence is the one of the first projects where one enters directly into the main space of the house. However, one does not immediately confront the view. The entry threshold is succinctly defined by a built-in cupboard and table. Foster then uses the same general plan organization as the Carling Residence, with the trajectory of the accommodation wing culminating in the "head" of the living room. In a measured sweep, Lautner rotates the simple monopitch roof about the central column of the main room, pivoting the movement of space to the outside. The encirclement of the roof turns the focus of the house to the view, and creates an opportunity to provide large expanses of glass and an outside terrace.

1953 › Bergren Residence
Hollywood, California

Left page:

Interior view of the living space
The living room floor is raised and detached from the nearside wall, creating what Lautner called a "free space".

Right:

The front terrace

Plan

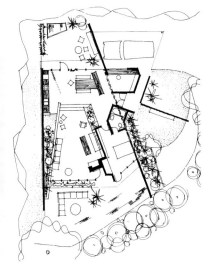

The Bergren Residence has free walls which angle open to the view below while enclosing a kitchen-dining room and outside patio behind. The walls, unusually, run perpendicular to the contour lines. The butterfly roof slopes down at an offset geometry to the shared main wall of the house, which provides an anchor for the raised floor of the living room. This floor is freed from the taller wall opposite as the ground level drops into an internal planted strip.

The bulk of the chimney increases as it gets higher, as the main wall of the house to which it is connected leans back. Through the weight of the chimney, complemented by the manipulation of the roof angles and floor levels, Lautner creates a hiatus to the outwards expulsion of space. The tension of this effect builds up under the low roof above the entrance and dining areas, reaching a crescendo as the roof rises over the living area. The result is a dynamic plan of eddies and currents, of both intimacy and spectacle, yet as in the contemporary buildings of Deutsch and Tyler, the observer is never left to simply confront the view.

1957 · Henry's Coffee Shop
Pomona, California

One of a series of diners designed to celebrate a post war zest for the car. Sited on Route 66 Lautner's 'landscape' for this building is that of highway, speed and headlights. These ephemeral qualities are referred to in the streamline elliptical plan. As with Pearlman, built the same year, the exterior atmosphere is drawn inside via the overhanging eaves and full height glazing to become an inextricable part of the interior high ceilinged space. The laminated timber roof structure is a strong and protective element, similar in theme to the cave-like interiors of Segel.

1957 · Pearlman Mountain Cabin
Idyllwild, California

Left page:
View from below

Right:
Main room

Plan

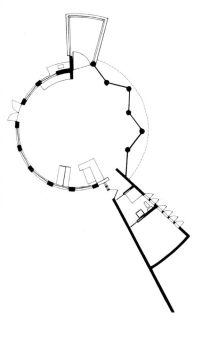

The Pearlman Mountain Cabin displays a new sense of muscularity. The material references to Wright, such as the use of horizontal boarding, are no longer evident. The house is a tough rendition of a mountain retreat—a cross between a log cabin and a tree house—and it is this expression to which the logs in the main elevation refer, rather than to some inadequate simulacrum of the forest beyond.

From below, Pearlman creates a new expression of the natural force of space flowing in and out, the main facade breaking satisfyingly free of the rules that its bent-open hairpin-like plan has set it. The angles and promontories of the building jut out from the hillside, the supporting poles exposed. The building has a sense of vital precipitousness, in self-conscious exposure to nature. The angles seem rough, the forms somewhat peculiar, yet the cabin still appears fresh, just conceived, propped on the site after Lautner's clear conception of it.

The zone of the faceted glass and sloping ceiling above create a wide band of transfer between inside and out: out coming in—in going out. The transparency of the envelope is accentuated by inserting the glass directly into the timber poles that support the living room cantilever. As Mrs Pearlman was a fine pianist the faceted glass envelope and sloping ceiling were designed with acoustics in mind.

1960 ▸ Malin Residence, "Chemosphere"
Hollywood, California

Standing on one column, the Malin Residence is a house that invites speculation, yet it is a considered solution to the problem of low budget and an unbuildably steep site. Its form recalls the toughness of a water tower.

Already the Pearlman Mountain Cabin consists of a single level platform raised completely free of the ground on columns—in the case of the Malin Residence on a single stalk. In this way Lautner overcame the unbuildable site, and left the landscape virtually untouched and therefore unspoilt. While disengaging from the ground in section, Lautner was also withdrawing from the surrounding landscape in plan. The wings of the supporting accommodation of Pearlman are truncated, while at Malin they are incorporated under the main roof altogether.

Access is by funicular from the carport below and via a bridge from the hillside, which the superstructure almost touches. In a completely new development, Lautner closes down the roof at the perimeter, protecting from the magnitude of the view. The transition to the outside is made through the edge detail.

This edge zone, while accommodating storage, a seat and at one point a small terrace, is also structural. The bowed laminated-timber roof supports, which also hold the glass, appear to slip away and out of the room, imbuing this place of change from inside to outside with weight. The thinness of the line of transition is in fact blurred into the whole threshold of angling sill and internal shelf, as the leaning glass shows almost no reflections. As at Pearlman, the effect of connecting very thin glass onto much bigger structural elements dematerializes the glass.

Plan

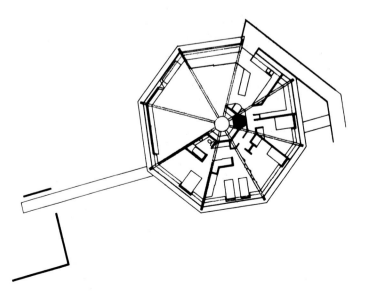

45

View from the hillside
Access to the Residence is by funicular.

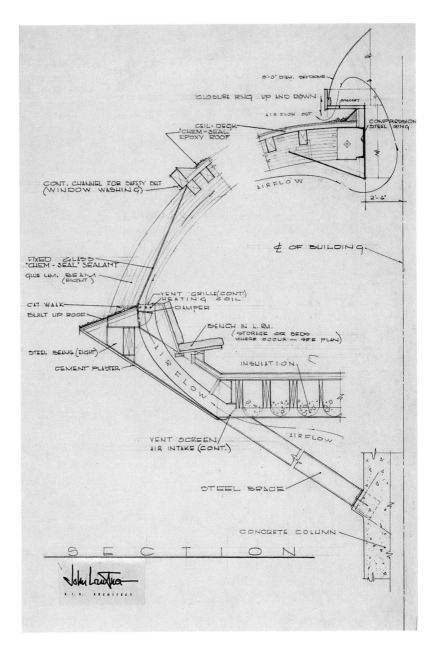

6'-0" DIAM. SKYDOME

CLOSURE RING - UP AND DOWN

AIR FLOW OUT

BRACKET

COMPRESSION STEEL RING

CEIL. DECK
"CHEM-SEAL"
EPOXY ROOF

AIRFLOW

2'-6"

CONT. CHANNEL FOR SAFETY BELT
(WINDOW WASHING)

℄ OF BUILDING.

FIXED GLASS
"CHEM-SEAL" SEALANT

GLUE LAM. BEAM
(EIGHT)

VENT GRILLE (CONT.)
HEATING COIL

CAT WALK

DAMPER

BUILT UP ROOF

BENCH IN L. RM.
(STORAGE OR BEDS
WHERE OCCUR — SEE PLAN)

STEEL BEAM (EIGHT)

INSULATION

AIRFLOW

CEMENT PLASTER

AIRFLOW

VENT SCREEN
AIR INTAKE (CONT.)

AIRFLOW

STEEL BRACE

CONCRETE COLUMN

S E C T I O N

John Lautner
A. I. A. ARCHITECT

Section
The edge detail accommodates storage and
a seat.

View from the living room towards the dining area and kitchen
The fireplace is to the hill side of the octagonal roof-light at the centre.

Right page:
Terrace
To eliminate vertigo, Lautner closed down the roof and thickened the perimeter upstand.

1961▸Wolff Residence
Hollywood, California

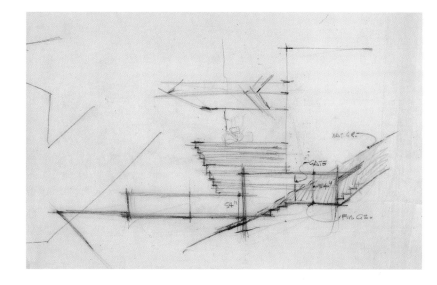

Section sketch

Because his client was impressed by the architecture of Frank Lloyd Wright, Lautner designed the Wolff Residence with Wright's trademark cantilevering hipped roofs. However, the way in which these copper-clad roofs are superimposed on the disjunct plans below is most unlike Wright. Instead, the building forms thrust and rotate out from the hillside in a series of juxtaposed and cascading rectangles, falling to the swimming pool below.

The heavy zigzag walls, built to withstand the soft site conditions and earthquakes, march out from the hillside, perpendicular to the contour but somehow contour-like. The projecting roofs and balconies weave between the foliage of the hillside, preserving four mature eucalyptus trees, and giving access to the different levels via secret paths. The trees continue to grow up through the bedroom and living room terraces, between glass and structure, and out above the roofs.

Wolff has comparatively few rooms, so Lautner had to use ingenuity to create a sense of expansiveness. In plan there are small outdoor terraces between the glass of the internal envelope and rocky walls. These protect the interior from the side view while connecting materially to the hillside. As gaps between the glass and stone they provide an important density or thickening of space, within the layering of each major room is set. In plan the smaller, intimate spaces at the back of each floor plate expand into the larger front rooms, and then into the view. In section the implied movement is caught between the shifting overhanging roofs above and jutting platforms and pool below, before flowing into the void. The combination of this flow of space in plan and section creates a dynamic spatial event.

At Wolff, Lautner developed a way of extending his idea of spatial projection to deal with an entire multi-tiered house by compounding its effect over various layers.

Entrance area that makes the transition between the low copper roadside roof to the surprise of the 16 foot high stone walls that dramatically structure the descending floor plates where the hillside falls away

This change is not simply the product of circular or hexagonal roof geometries, or the steepness of a site. Lautner changed his attitude decisively: no longer were the buildings joined with the landscape, but rather they were separated from it.

Plan

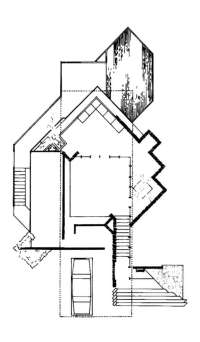

1962▸Garcia Residence
Los Angeles, California

The Garcia Residence seems at first to be a one-liner: an overarching roof structure
with accommodation filling in below. Yet it has subtleties and surprises, starting with
one's introduction to the house from the carport, entered at road-level at the back
where it nestles high up under the roof. A spiral staircase from the carport level
descends, still under the roof, to give entrance to the private accommodation on one
side and the public wing on the other.

The building is propped off the ground by two V-shaped supports at the front
giving it the appearance of floating just above the hillside undergrowth. A terrace
swells out from circulatory area, providing alternative entries to the living room and
dining wing where its billowing effect is balanced by a tilt at the end of the curving roof.
A feeling of space dissipating out from the centre is also developed using the step drop
to the living room from the dining room as the roof squeezes down on the accommodation, matching a similar step drop in the master bedroom. The long span form of the
steel roof piece was to develop further in Lautner's later work to become two-way
curving concrete roof structures, a signature of his projects Silvertop and Elrod.

There is a lightness and sense of fun to this building. The simple structure is
animated by the movement of the circulation, the rhythm of the plan and glazed elevation. Little wonder that the client was a jazz musician.

Living room
The kitchen is located behind the low wall with
inbuilt seating at the end of the room.

Right:
Section

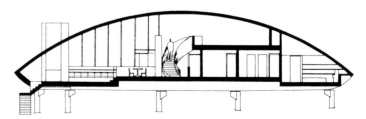

View from below
The long span steel frame of the roof allows
flexibility in the organization of the interior, as
the partitions are not load-bearing.

Right:
Plan

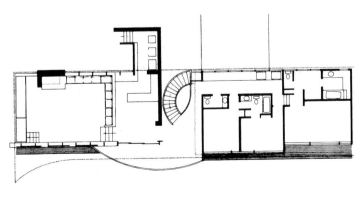

1963 ▸ Reiner Residence, "Silvertop"
Los Angeles, California

Left page:
View across the swimming pool to the music room

The ten years of designing and constructing "Silvertop", always under analysis by a consultant team and his client's exacting eye, must have been stifling. However, Reiner's unlimited budget gave Lautner the opportunity to test and innovate new building systems. At "Silvertop" Lautner also "discovered" concrete, the ideal medium for the spaces he was seeking to make, being both "solid and free".

The pool is detailed with an "overflowing edge" to merge seamlessly with the view of Silver Lake below. The shapes of the roofs create a "new hilltop".

Plan

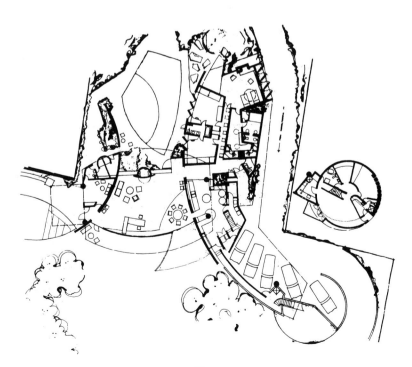

Sliding door to the living room
Reiner specially developed a flexible screw-drive to
propel the sliding door along its curving path.

Right page:
Living room
The hangers suspending the frameless glass were
produced in Reiner's own workshops.

The house from the tennis courts
The guest house is located in the rotunda enclosed by the vehicular access ramp. Above the guest house, on the same level as the main house, are the carports and, to the left, the kitchen.

Bathroom to the master bedroom
The wall to the left adjoins a planted triangular space allowing light into the bathroom but preserving its privacy. Floors are terrazzo and walls are lined with marble.

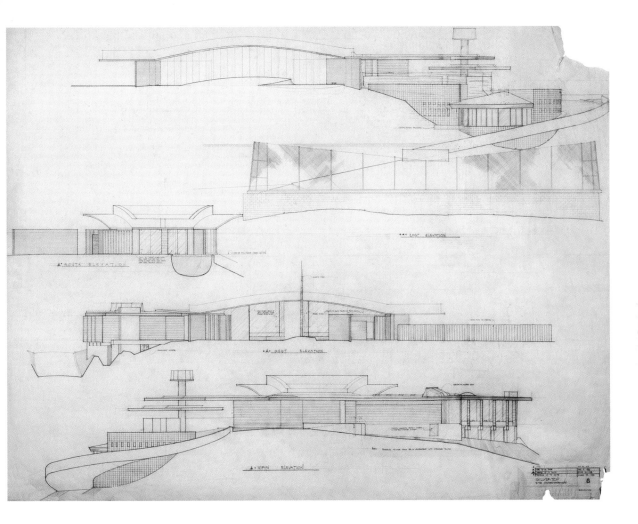

Elevation drawings

Living room area with view of fireplace
A planted court is located behind the fireplace.

1968 ▸ Elrod Residence
Palm Springs, California

The Elrod Residence has many apparent similarities to the Carling Residence—the trailing wing of accommodation, the centralized main space under a tent-like roof —yet in Elrod the sense of enclosure is more akin to Pearlman and Malin. In the intervening years between Carling and Elrod, Lautner had built some 50 buildings including "Silvertop", which honed his ability to technically realize what he had in mind for a particular site.

The Elrod Residence is a masterful use of concrete that allowed Lautner to create long spans and to mould spaces from a material expressive of itself. In a sense the Elrod Residence marks a turning point in the development of his architecture which leads to the extravagant flowing forms of the Segel Residence (1979).

Elrod is somewhat like a military bunker from the road, or when viewed from the slope below. However, the main space, with its 60ft diameter, clear-span roof, opens up like a desert flower to the sky above, with light penetrating the space through the angled sun protectors of the roof. The chamfers to the edges of these openings accentuate the thickness of the concrete shell, beautifully made by an old contractor of Wright's, Wally Niewiadomski. The delicate thickness of the edge beam, brought down close to the encircling patterned floor of slate, contrasts with this weight, and the sense is of the roof of the main space being lifted off.

The floors are cut down into the rock so that the bigger boulders are at roof height. The landscape is literally brought into the house as wall, screen or furniture. Frameless glass is inserted between rock and concrete structure to create the envelope, undulating to animate the internal space and follow the shifting floor level. The main exit to the outside is under the roof, but hidden from view behind a boulder, where steps lead through to the terrace and pool, onto concrete steps cantilevering out of the wall of the pool—reminiscent of the leaves of the roof structure—down to the rocky hillside.

At night the black slate throws no reflection, and from the seating area on the circular carpet in the living room, the view of stars and lights in the valley, which twinkle in the reflection of the pool, must seem a special performance seen from a private island.

View of the living room looking out to the night view
At night the circular carpet appears to float on the black slate floor, dramatizing the display of the lights of Palm Springs in the valley below.

Right:
Section through bedroom, living room and pool

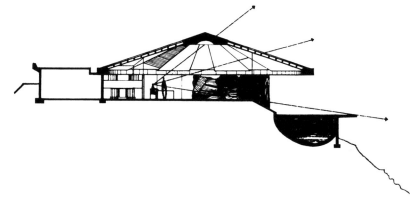

View of the conical concrete roof of the main space of the Elrod Residence from the entry court on the street side of the house
The segmental glass clerestories of the roof are protected from the western sun.

Right:
Plan

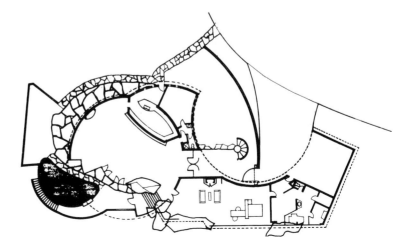

1968 ▸ Stevens Residence
Malibu, California

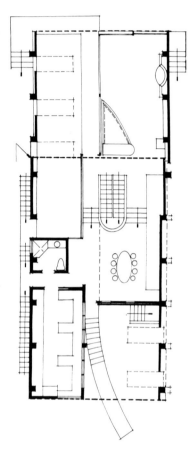

The demands of the Stevens Residence inspired Lautner to develop a new form of organization. Unlike his previous hillside or hilltop sites, this building is located on a difficult, narrow lot on the edge of the Malibu beach. Lautner was required to build a house with upwards of 12 rooms yet also open it up to the views: mountain at the rear, sea at the front. His solution was to create two opposed concrete catenary shells. The roofs are monolithic and structurally rational, requiring a minimum of support and upkeep. Instead of being sited on topography, they are the topography: two waves.

The roof enclosure is colonized by a second structure of wooden floors and wall divisions. The dialectic between the opposing curves is resolved in the central passageway that runs through the house on each floor, and in the stairs, which are the centrepiece from which the wooden internal structure grows. The inside of the concrete shells runs through uncluttered and exposed.

There is none of the thickening of the end facades that takes place at Pearlman or Baldwin, between the interior and the view. Instead, the house is internalized: its main axis of view is back on itself, a view to infinity of the curve of the roof. The views to mountain and sea on either side are subsidiary to the life of the family and protection from the beach environment.

Plan

Left page:
Lap pool
Translucent glass elements diffuse the light entering through the openings in the concrete structure and give privacy from the neighbouring property, while also helping to provide protection from the seaside wind.

Living room, looking out to the sea
The lap pool is located to the left.

Right page:
**Beach elevation, showing one concrete
catenary shell structure in the foreground
and the other in the background**
The living room and master bedroom above
it look out to sea views.

1969·Walstrom Residence
Los Angeles, California

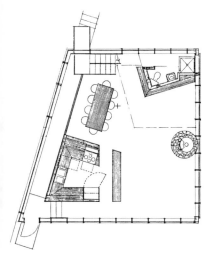

Main level plan

The Walstrom house is set within the trees and foliage of the steep hillside on which it is sited, but held off the ground to allow the landscape to continue uninterrupted beneath it. The roof opens up to the view beyond, a dramatic counterpoint to the downward force of the slope, yet to either side large areas of glass introduce greenery into the house. This tree-house quality is carried through into the interior, whose fine plan incorporates a kitchen within the main room with the strong shape of a toilet block and storage area balancing the dynamic of forces around the room.

The two bedrooms below raise the living room on a platform into the treetops. Enormous sheet glass windows border the space that joins both levels, looking back on the leafy, restful view of the hillside behind.

Walstrom is a fairly unusual building for Lautner. It has echoes of other houses, recalling both the large envelopes that started with Segel and the terrace-like buildings epitomized by Arango. It is part of the beginning of Lautner's mature period and evinces poise, balance and assuredness. It is a quietly unique building, one which its clients reported as a "sculptural work of art".

1973▸Arango Residence
Acapulco, Mexico

Left page:

View from below, looking to master bedroom

Right:

Design sketch, showing sun angles and reflection pool behind the bedrooms

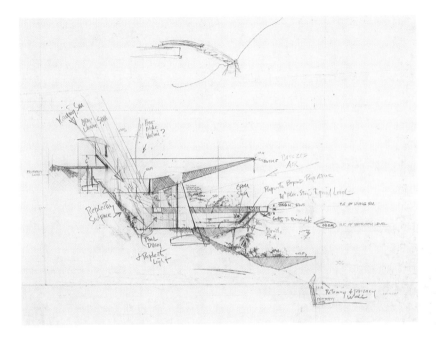

Arango, deservedly one of Lautner's most celebrated buildings, is sited on a steep hillside above the Acapulco Bay. The closest comparable project to Arango is the Pearlman Mountain Cabin, built some 15 years earlier.

The comparison to Pearlman is important, as the Cabin—together with some other projects of the late 1950s and early 1960s—marked the beginning of Lautner's mature work. The peaked roof and truncated, enclosed wing of accommodation at Pearlman see their reflection at Arango, albeit on a vastly greater scale. The grittiness of Pearlman, with its jutting geometries and rough wood edges, is enlarged in the medium of concrete to achieve the forcefulness necessary to match the view.

At Arango the main living area is in the air, on the terrace of unpolished marble, amidst a landscape of sparse concrete furniture only. The terrace is pushed up by the plinth of bedroom accommodation below, and supported to the side by the service block. On the terrace the facade of Pearlman is done away with, the architecture stripped down and enlarged until it is pure spectacle. The envelope of the meandering moat replaces a handrail, the roof supports are vestiges of walls, and the peak of the great concrete roof—a massive version of the upward turn of the Pearlman ceiling—angles outwards from the terrace in both an embracing and a declamatory gesture.

Terrace, serving as outdoor living and dining area

The moat keeps out crawling insects and eliminates the need for a handrail. The meandering water blends with the water of the bay below.

Exposed hillside and protected terrace behind the bedrooms

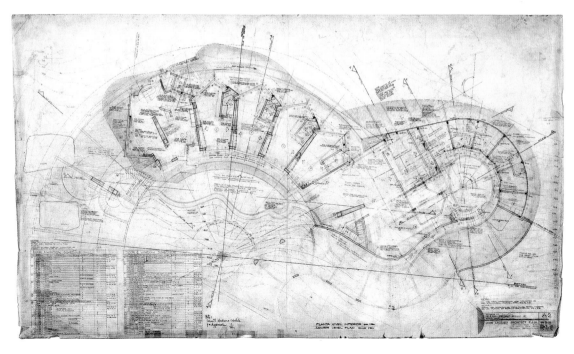

1979 · Segel Residence
Malibu, California

The Segel Residence has the low triangular living space of Beyer and Shearing set against the double height space of the subsidiary accommodation. Contained under two roofs, a lower grass-covered concrete shell encloses the main living space, over which the higher roof swoops. The two create a protective profile, building up from the seashore to culminate in an extraordinary, sharp-edged peak at the rear of the house. This profile is extended to enclose beneath its caul a protected swimming pool and an outdoor courtyard to the rear for parking and parties. Lautner's concept for the house is a cave, protecting the inhabitants from the noise of the highway and high winds.

The intimacy of the interior appears to contradict the exterior. Warm, ship-like timber boarding is used extensively inside. Slots in the boarding admit stripes of light onto the curving walls, enhancing the sense of cavern-like protectiveness. Outside, the large expanses of full-height glazing become one monolithic entity with the roof and concrete outcroppings of stair and chimney, obscuring the real size of the building. In plan, entry is through a slot in the high, windowless wall of the rear, all allusive to the idea of a cave.

Beyer and Segel are built on sites exposed to extremes of weather. In these projects the depth of the roof replaces the thickened envelope of Malin and Pearlman. The transition between inside and outside occurs now in the section of the roof, as implied by its revealed edge. This act of enclosure gives the visual weight necessary to balance the force of the elements.

View of the terrace court, showing how the rear of the house finishes off in a peak
The blank walls of the rear of the house provide protection from the noise of the adjoining highway.

Left page:
Master bedroom

Segel Residence seen from the beach
The living room in the foreground abuts the
double-story accommodation of kitchen, guest
room and garage on the ground floor, and master
bedroom, office, dance studio and maid's room
on the upper floor. Views of the sea from the
second floor are over the grassed concrete roof of
the living room.

Left:
Plan

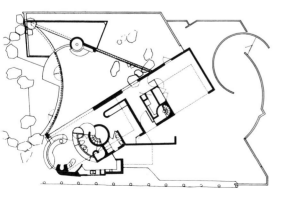

1983 · Beyer Residence
Malibu, California

The Beyer Residence incorporates itself in the shoreline, with the prow of the terrace pushing into the sea. Beneath the freeform roof the furniture of the living spaces is arranged, rockpool-like, in between boulders and off-shutter concrete walls: the living room is in the view. In this house there is a sectional gradation of light and enclosure. This spatial progression develops from the protected, hidden support rooms of bathroom, kitchen, and courtyard, via an upperlevel loft, half secluded from the panorama and pushing up towards the slotted rooflights in the ceiling. These spaces then give way to a widening and heightening of the main living volume, culminating in the ultimate transition to the openness of sea and horizon. Once again Lautner found his leitmotiv: disappearing space.

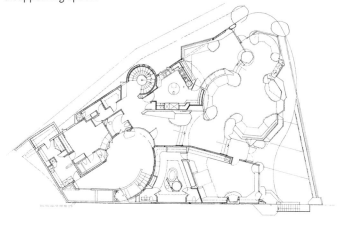

1963/1989 ▸ Sheats Residence

Los Angeles, California ▸ Remodelled for Mr Jim Goldstein, 1989

Sheats was built in 1963, some 14 years after Lautner's 1949 Schaffer Residence. The two share the same hourglass shape, with a plan gathered in at the entrance area, and movement pushed to the sides by the position of the fireplace. The pathway at Sheats, instead of filtering into the woods, moves out from the hillside at an angle, and joins the triangular plans of the house together in the entrance area and dining room. It then steps down to the lower level master bedroom to its corner full-height revelation of the view. Along this route there are two other culminating spaces: the dining room and the main living room.

Where Schaffer has a private garden enclosed to the rear, at Sheats this position is occupied by the accommodation wing. The bulk of these rooms is hidden by the perspectival trick of the triangle narrowing to the dining room, where the observer is unaware of the number of rooms hidden between the diverging perimeter glazed-wall passageways on either side. The sense of divergence, of escape outside, is reinforced by the low, timber-boarded ceiling. Only above the kitchen and dining room table, whose cantilevered glass set in slanting blocks of concrete fits with the triangle shards of the plan, are large skylights opened in the roof, holding the dissipation of space to the outside.

The living room is part of a platform between the upward slope of the hill and the pathway to the master bedroom. It is situated in the plan between the waterfall pool at the entrance and the trapezoid swimming pool in front. Large areas of flatness are created, stretching out from the hillside, through the glassy facade over the reflecting water to the slight inclination at the platform's edge, at the apex of the triangle, to elide into the view without a handrail. Generated from the chimney is the great triangular coffered roof, which covers the front of the living room and part of the pool, angling the focus of the living room to the view.

The roof, thick edged and enclosing, contrasts dramatically with the simple planes of the ground surfaces, water and minimal interior furniture below. Instead it belongs more to the fecundity of the planting of the hillside, from which it is supported on one side, and the treetops into which the living room is visually swept. It is as if the forest canopy of Schaffer needed to be recorded in something more substantial than an agglomeration of separate roofs.

The Sheats roof, in its angular geometric form, is representative of a wild space, a place in a forest or natural grove. This is the space, discovered when Lautner was a boy, for which he continually yearned, and which he strove to rediscover through the techniques of architecture. It yearns on now in the beholder's eye. The interior is speckled by the light, the moving light on the ground in the primeval forest, made by 750 drinking glasses set as skylights into the concrete of the roof.

View from under the coffered concrete living
room roof to the pool and view of Los Angeles
below

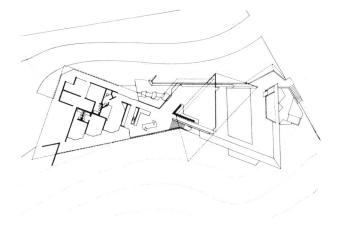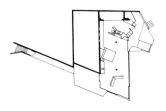

Lower-level plan (right), main level plan (left)

The master bedroom after Lautner's remodel
The glass at the corner slides open under remote
control.

Living room, looking towards entrance pool

Left:
Carport

Bar and dining area
The living room is on the left.

Right:
Bathroom, master bedroom, after remodel
The windows to the rear look up into the water of
the pool.

Life and Work

1911 ▶ John Edward Lautner born 16 July,
Marquette, Michigan. Eldest child of Vida
Cathleen Gallagher and John Edward Lautner

1933 ▶ Lautner graduates from Northern State
Teachers College (now called Northern Michigan
University) with a degree in English.

1934 ▶ Lautner marries Mary F. Roberts.
Lautner is accepted as an apprentice by Frank
Lloyd Wright at Taliesin.
Lautner and Mary live at Taliesin together.

1938 ▶ Daughter Karol Lautner born

1940 ▶ Lautner leaves Taliesin and Frank Lloyd
Wright to start his own practice.
Lautner Residence, Los Angeles
Bell Residence, Los Angeles
Springer Residence, Los Angeles

1942 ▶ Son Michael John Lautner born
Astor Farm, Indio

1944 ▶ Daughter Mary Beecher Lautner born

1945
Darrow Office Building, Beverly Hills
Hancock Residence, Los Angeles
Weinstein Remodel, Los Angeles

1946 ▶ Daughter Judith Munroe Lautner born
Eisele Guest House, Los Angeles
Mauer Residence, Los Angeles

1947 ▶ Lautner and Mary divorce
Carling Residence, Los Angeles
Desert Hot Springs Motel, Desert Hot Springs
Gantvoort Residence, Flintridge
Henry's Restaurant, Glendale
Jacobsen Residence, Hollywood
Polin Residence, Hollywood
Eisele Ski Cabin, Big Bear (project)

1948 ▶ Lautner marries Elizabeth Gilman
Honnold. Step-daughter Elizabeth Honnold (born
1931)
Lincoln Mercury Showroom, Glendale
Sheats Apartments (L'Horizon), Los Angeles

Valley Escrow Offices, Sherman Oaks
Abbot Apartments, Los Angeles (project)
William Adams Residence, Pasadena (project)
Ferber Residence, Altadena (project)
Mayer Residence, Pacific Palisades (project)
Ross Residence, Los Angeles (project)
Stiff Residence, Los Angeles (project)

1949
Dahlstrom Residence, Pasadena
Googies Coffee House, Los Angeles
UPA Studios, Burbank
Schaffer Residence, Montrose
Brooks Addition, Studio City (project)

1950
Alexander Residence, Long Beach
Foster Residence, Sherman Oaks
Harvey Residence, Los Angeles
Shusett Residence, Beverly Hills
Monroe Residence, Los Angeles (project)
Noerdlinger Residence, Playa Del Rey (project)

1951
Baxter-Hodiak Remodel, Los Angeles
Bick Residence, Brentwood
Evans and Reeves Exhibition Stand, Los Angeles
Lippett Remodel, Los Angeles

1952
Carr Residence, Los Angeles
Gootgeld Residence, Beverly Hills
Howe Residence, Los Angeles
Williams Residence, Hollywood
Ewing Residence, Los Angeles (project)

1953
Bergren Residence, Hollywood
Henry's Restaurant Remodel, Pasadena
Payne Addition, San Dimas
Tyler Residence, Studio City
Leipziger Remodel, Beverly Hills (project)
Pittenger Residence, Los Angeles (project)

1954
Beachwood Market, Hollywood
Coneco Corporation House, Los Angeles
Fischer Residence, Los Angeles
Lek Remodel, Studio City

John Lautner explains one of his projects.

Deutsch Residence, Hollywood

1955
Baldwin Residence, Los Angeles
Henry's Restaurant Addition, Arcadia

1956
Harpel Residence, Hollywood
Seletz Studio, Los Angeles
Speer Contractors Office Building, Los Angeles
Crenshaw Methodist Church, Los Angeles
(project)

1957
Henry's Restaurant, Pomona
Pearlman Residence, Idyllwild
Zahn Residence, Hollywood

1958
Kaynar Factory for K. Reiner, Pico Rivera
Hatherall Residence, Sun Valley
Dolley Apartments, Laguna Beach (project)
Pearlman Residence, Santa Ana (project)
Sawyer Mountain Cabin, Los Angeles (project)
Sheanin Residence, Los Angeles (project)
Lindenberg Residence, Sherman Oaks (project)

1959
Henry's Restaurant, Alhambra
Henry's Restaurant, Santa Ana
Ernest Lautner Residence, Pensacola, Florida
Olin Office Building, Claremont (project)
Glazier Residence, Los Angeles (project)

1960
Concannon Residence, Beverly Hills
Malin Residence ("Chemosphere"), Hollywood
Midtown School, Los Angeles
Chapel of World Peace, Dedicated to Dr Martin
Luther King, Los Angeles (project)

1961
Preminger Swimming Pool, Los Angeles
Tolstoy Residence, Alta Loma
Offices on 1777 North Vine Street, Los Angeles
Wolff Residence, Hollywood
Akers Residence, Malibu (project)

1962
Garcia Residence, Los Angeles
Henry's Restaurant Addition, Glendale
Thiele Addition to the Coneco Corporation
House, Los Angeles (project)
Martel Residence, Los Angeles (project)
Shusett Office Building, Los Angeles (project)

1963
Sheats Residence, Los Angeles
Reiner Residence ("Silvertop"), Los Angeles
Wolff Remodel, Los Angeles
Ballet School and Theatre, San Diego (project)
Fell Residence, Beverly Hills (project)
Mann Residence, Huntington Harbor (project)
Morris Residence, Los Angeles (project)
Exhibition at Mount San Antonio College,
Walnut, California

1964
Conrad Addition, Fullerton
Henry's Restaurant Addition, Alhambra
Residence for Bay Cities Mortgages, Palos Verdes
(project)
Bisharat Residence, Los Angeles (project)
Fink Residence, Los Angeles (project)
Goldsmith Residence, Los Angeles (project)

1965
Stanley Johnson Residence, Laguna Beach
Clark Residence, Los Angeles (project)
Newport Research Center, Newport Beach
(project)
Rosen Parking Building, Los Angeles (project)

1966
Marina View Heights Headquarters, San Juan
Capistrano
Harpel Residence, Anchorage, Alaska
Moser Residence, Oakview (project)
Exhibition at the University of Kentucky,
Lexington, Kentucky

1967
Exhibition at the California State College, Los
Angeles

1968
Elrod Residence, Palm Springs
Henry's Restaurant Addition, Glendale
Stevens Residence, Malibu Bay Colony
Zimmerman Residence, Studio City
Motor Inn Motel for Glenn Amundson, Glendale
(project)
Laboratory and Living Quarters for Owens
Valley Observatory, Cal Tech (project)
Peters Residence, Thousand Oaks (project)
Robertson Residence, Lake Hollywood
(project)
Walker Residence, Los Angeles (project)

1969
Mills Addition, Flintridge
Walstrom Residence, Los Angeles
HUD Project for Low Cost Housing (project)

1970
Garwood Residence, Malibu
Science Building, Hilo Campus, University of
Hawaii

1971
Familian Residence, Beverly Hills
Busustow Cabin, Lake Alamnor
Lueck Residence, San Diego (project)
Moen Residence, Laguna Beach (project)
Raintree Inn for Dan Stevens, Grand Junction,
Colorado (project)

1973
Arango Residence, Acapulco, Mexico
Jordan Residence, Laguna Beach
Franklyn Residence, Buenos Aires, Argentina
(project)

Dr Little Dental Clinic, San Juan Capistrano
(project)

1974
Nichols Residence, Farmington, New Mexico
(project)
Doumani Duplex, Marina Del Rey (project)
Hurd Residence, Horseshoe Bay, Texas (project)
John Lautner Mountain Cabin, Three Rivers,
California (project)
Lucy Residence, Horseshoe Bay, Texas (project)
Rosenthal Residence, Las Vegas, Nevada
(project)
Three Worlds of Los Angeles, Exhibition,
sponsored by United States Information Service
and Cultural Centers in Europe. Curated by
Beata Inaya

1975
Marco Wolff Mountain Cabin, Idyllwild
Burrell Ranch, Grayson County
Nature Center, Griffith Park, Los Angeles

1976
Curtiss Residence, Hunting Valley, Ohio (project)
Familian Beach House, Malibu (project)
Starr Residence, Bell Canyon (project)
Los Angeles Twelve, Exhibition at the Pacific
Design Center, Los Angeles, and at the California
State Polytechnic University, Pomona

1977
Aldrich Remodel, Los Angeles
Cavalier Motel for Dan Stevens, Los Angeles
(project)
Hellinger Residence, Pacific Palisades (project)

1978
Aita Addition for Private Discotheque, Los
Angeles (project)
Pavilion for the Edward Dean Museum, Cherry
Valley (project)

1979 ▶ Lautner's wife Elizabeth dies.
Crippled Children's Society Rehabilitation Center,
Woodland Hills
Segel Residence, Malibu
Hope Residence, Palm Springs

1980
Crahan Swimming Pool, Los Angeles
Rawlins Residence, Newport Beach
Bornstein Residence, Los Angeles (project)

1981
Celestial Arts Office Remodel, Millbrea (project)
Ellersieck Residence, Altadena (project)
Lynn Residence, Santa Barbara (project)
Turner Condominiums, Marina Del Rey (project)

1982 ▶ Lautner marries Francisca Hernandez.
'Flowers That Bloom In the Spring, Tra La',
Flower Shop for Dan Stevens, Los Angeles
Turner Residence, Aspen, Colorado
Schwimmer Residence, Los Angeles
Krause Residence, Malibu
Zimmerman Residence Addition, Studio City
(project)

1983
Beyer Residence, Malibu

1985
Exhibition at the Schindler House, Los Angeles

1986
Roven Residence, Beverly Hills (project)

1987
Nicholas Addition, Beverly Hills

1988
Haagen Beach Cabin, Malibu (project)

1989
Boykoff Remodel, Los Angeles
Goldstein Offices, Los Angeles
Goldstein Remodel of Sheats Residence, Los
Angeles
Todd Addition to Hancock Residence, Los Angeles
Walter Remodel of Concannon Residence, Beverly
Hills (project)

1990
Private Residence, California
Yokeno Residence, Pacific Palisades
Miles Davis Swimming Pool, Malibu (project)
Townsend Residence, Malibu (project)

1991
Eicher Remodel of Carling Residence, Los Angeles
Marina Fine Arts, Marina Del Rey
Architecture as Art, Exhibition at the
Athenaeum, La Jolla
John Lautner, Exhibition at the Hochschule für
Angewandte Kunst, Wien. Curated by Johannes
Kraus and Hubert Klumpner
John Lautner, Exhibition at the Harvard
Graduate School of Design, Harvard University,
Cambridge, Massachusetts
John Lautner, Exhibition at the Graham
Foundation for Advanced Studies in the Fine
Arts, Chicago, Illinois

1992
Shearing Residence, Coronado Cays
Friedberg-Rodman Remodel of Zahn Residence,
Los Angeles
Exhibition at the Emily Carr College of Art and
Design, Vancouver
Exhibition at the National Institute of
Architectural Education, New York

1993
Worchell Remodel of Bell Residence, Los Angeles
(project)—in progress when Lautner died
Johns Studio, Los Angeles (project)—in progress
when Lautner died
Berns Remodel of Jordan Residence, Laguna
Beach (project)—in progress when Lautner died
Wood Residence, Malibu (project)—in progress
when Lautner died

1994 ▶ John Lautner dies 24 October in Los
Angeles.
John Lautner Foundation established
Whiting Residence, Sun Valley, Idaho (project)—
in progress when Lautner died
John Lautner: California Architect. Selected
Projects 1937–1991, Exhibition at the School of
Architecture Gallery, Princeton University

Montrose Flintridge

Sherman Oaks

Hollywood

Malibu

Los Angeles Pomona

PACIFIC OCEAN

94

Desert
Hot Springs o

Palm Springs o

Idyllwild o

California

Desert Hot Springs
Desert Hot Springs Motel

Flintridge
Gantvoort Residence

Hollywood
Bergren Residence
Malin Residence, "Chemosphere"
Wolff Residence

Idyllwild
Pearlman Mountain Cabin

Los Angeles
Carling Residence
Garcia Residence
Lautner Residence
Mauer Residence
Reiner Residence, "Silvertop"
Sheats Residence
Walstrom Residence

Malibu
Beyer Residence
Segel Residence
Stevens Residence

Montrose
Schaffer Residence

Palm Springs
Elrod Residence

Pomona
Henry's Coffee Shop

Sherman Oaks
Foster Residence

Acknowledgements

We would like to thank the following people for their help in preparation of this book:
Frances Anderton, Helena Arahuete, Peter Blundell-Jones, Rory Campbell-Lange, Frank Escher, Don Higgins, Elizabeth Honnold, Kezia Lange, Victoria Larson, Judy Lautner, Karol Lautner Peterson, Michael Moore, Duncan Nicholson, Julius Shulman, Julia Strickland, Alan Weintraub

Bibliography

▶ Campbell-Lange, Barbara-Ann: John Lautner. Unpublished interview, 10th December 1990

▶ Cohen, Bette Jane: The Spirit in Architecture, John Lautner. Documentary film written and directed by Bette Jane Cohen, produced by Bette Jane Cohen and Evelyn Wendel, 1991

▶ Escher, Frank (ed.): John Lautner, Architect. Artemis London Limited, London, 1994

▶ Hess, Alan: The Architecture of John Lautner. Rizzoli International Publications, Inc., New York, 1999

▶ Lautner, John: Lecture given at SCI-Arc Los Angeles, 23rd January 1991

▶ Pendro, Roland James: Solid and Free: the Architecture of John Lautner. Unpublished thesis, University of California, Los Angeles, 1987

▶ Wahlroos, Ingalill: John Lautner. Unpublished interview for UCLA Architecture Journal, 29th November 1989

Credits